Read All About Dogs

DOGS WITH A JOB

Barbara J. Patten

The Rourke Corporation, Inc.
Vero Beach, Florida 32964

PHOTO CREDITS
Photos courtesy of Corel

Library of Congress Cataloging-in-Publication Data

Patten, Barbara J., 1951-
   Dogs with a job / by Barbara J. Patten.
      p. cm. — (Read all about dogs)
   Includes index.
   Summary: Illustrations and brief text present various breeds of working dogs, including collies, sheepdogs, and huskies.
    ISBN 0-86593-456-8
    1. Working dogs—Juvenile literature.   [1. Working dogs   2. Dogs.]
I. Title II. Series: Patten, Barbara J., 1951- Read all about dogs.
SF428.2.P37   1996
636.7'3—dc20   96–23070
                                                              CIP
                                                               AC

Printed in the USA

TABLE OF CONTENTS

BOXERS AND GERMAN SHEPHERDS

Different in looks, but showing the same courage and strength, boxers and **German shepherds** (JER mun) (SHEP erdz) have always worked side by side.

These dogs served in World Wars I and II as guards and supply and message carriers. They also helped find missing soldiers.

Known for intelligence, German shepherds are trained for many jobs.

Looking like "tough guys," boxers are really big babies around the house.

Boxers and German shepherds are often used as guide dogs for the blind. Their large size, attentiveness, and ability to be trained have suited them well for this important job.

Many boxers and German shepherds work at winning love as family pets. Both are loyal and affectionate dogs who work and play hard and enjoy being part of a family.

COLLIES

Most of us know the **collie** (KAHL ee) as "Lassie" from the movies and television. The Lassie stories of canine courage and intelligence tell us about this special breed.

Collies are hard-working farm dogs. They herd, or help move flocks of sheep, to grazing areas, keeping them together and out of danger. Long, thick fur keeps collies warm in winter.

Collies take herding seriously. Gentle family pets have been known to "herd" a child away from danger the same way working collies move sheep.

The collie's thick coat should be brushed every day.

WELSH CORGIS

Fearless and sure of themselves, **Welsh corgis** (WELSH) (KAWR geez) don't seem to notice that they stand only 10 to 12 inches tall.

First seen in the country of Wales, corgis have worked for hundreds of years herding both horses and cattle. Their unusual method of getting these large animals to move has earned them the nickname "heelers."

Corgis run up to cows or horses, nip at their heels, and then drop flat on the ground to avoid being kicked. It seems to work. The big animals move along, and the corgis appear to enjoy the challenge.

Welsh corgis are called "heelers" because they nip at the heels of cattle.

Woodson

OLD ENGLISH SHEEPDOGS

With a coat so shaggy you may wonder if there is a dog inside, the Old English sheepdog bounces happily through life.

These dogs were first seen in England. They worked, herding sheep and cattle to market.

Sheepdogs need a lot of brushing. In return they are faithful, protective, and fun.

Yes, Old English sheepdogs can see through all that hair.

GREAT DANES

With the body size of a small pony, a **Great Dane** (GRAYT DAYN) is hard to miss—anywhere.

Years ago, hunters used Great Danes to hunt wild pigs. Today, this friendly canine makes a good house guard and family pet.

Everyone moves over when a Great Dane lies down!

SAMOYEDS

The hard-working, snow-white Samoyed is a hardy dog. From Siberia, a vast frozen area of Western Russia, Samoyeds have fluffy, thick coats that keep them warm in the coldest weather.

Pads of thick hair between their toes give them "snowshoe feet." They can walk long distances comfortably through snow and ice.

Samoyeds worked herding reindeer in the Northland and are famous for pulling dog sleds in the Arctic and Antarctic snowfields. Medium in size, they weigh 40 to 60 pounds.

After a hard day's work, this Samoyed is ready for dinner.

SIBERIAN HUSKIES

The speedy, stubborn **Siberian husky** (sy BEER ee un) (HUS kee) was brought to the U.S. from Russia to "mush," or pull, in dog sled races. As these handsome dogs outraced other dog teams in long, hard competitions, they became very popular.

Racing for sport is just part of the husky's history. They have always been hard-working sled dogs, moving people and supplies across the frozen North.

Some Siberian huskies have beautiful blue eyes.

NEWFOUNDLANDS AND SAINT BERNARDS

Newfoundlands (NOO fun lundz) and **Saint Bernards** (SAYNT) (ber NAHRDZ) are gentle giants and life-saving heroes.

Newfoundlands, a favorite dog of sailors and fishermen, have webbed feet, excellent for swimming. These canine lifeguards have rescued many adults and children from the northern sea.

Although happier in water than pulling a cart, Newfoundlands are used for many tasks.

This Newfoundland pup has a lot of growing to do to look like mom!

Saint Bernards lived high in the mountains of Europe. They are said to have rescued over 2,000 travelers lost in dangerous snowstorms and snowslides, or avalanches.

The Saint Bernard's keen nose can follow a person's scent over long distances. Sharp hearing allows the dog to warn people of avalanches before the humans themselves can hear the sound.

LET'S THANK THESE DOGS

Today, many working dogs have retired to become family pets. Many, though, still earn their dinner looking out for their masters.

Like people, dogs need clean water, good food, medical care, and a warm, safe place to sleep in order to stay healthy and strong.

Police dogs, seeing-eye dogs, farm dogs, and family dogs all put their trust in the people around them. It is our job to care for them.

The kind face of the bearded collie wins many hearts.

GLOSSARY

canine (KAY nyn) — of or about dogs; like a dog

collie (KAHL ee) — a long-haired, narrow-faced dog used for herding

Great Dane (GRAYT DAYN) — very large, powerful dog with short smooth coat, and narrow head

German shepherd (JER mun) (SHEP erd) — a large dog with thick gray, brown, or black coat; also called "police" and "seeing-eye" dog

Newfoundland (NOO fun lund) — a strong dog with thick, black coat. An excellent swimmer

Siberian husky (sy BEER ee un) (HUS kee) — a big dog with heavy coat of different colors, often used to pull sleds

Saint Bernard (SAYNT) (ber NAHRD) — a strong, brown-and-white dog known for rescuing people from snowstorms

Welsh corgi (WELSH) (KAWR gee) — a dog from Wales that has a long body, short legs, and a face like a fox

When the wind blows, you can see the eyes of an Old English sheepdog.

INDEX